My Name is Cletus

CANDY & CLETUS STOOKSBURY

CrossBooks™
A Division of LifeWay
1663 Liberty Drive
Bloomington, IN 47403
www.crossbooks.com
Phone: 1-866-879-0502

First published by CrossBooks 12/21/2010

ISBN: 978-1-6150-7686-4 (sc)

Printed in the United States of America

This book is printed on acid-free paper.

Any people depicted in stock imagery provided by Thinkstock are models, and such images are being used for illustrative purposes only.

Certain stock imagery © Thinkstock.

Because of the dynamic nature of the Internet, any Web addresses or links contained in this book may have changed since publication and may no longer be valid. The views expressed in this work are solely those of the author and do not necessarily reflect the views of the publisher, and the publisher hereby disclaims any responsibility for them.

CROSSBOOKS
PUBLISHING

This Book Belongs To:

 _____

- Chapter 1 -

A New Home

It was very lonely in the pet store. I wondered if anyone would ever adopt me. All of the other puppies made fun of my long ears and nose and they said my feet were too big. Day after day I watched the other puppies picked out by people, who took them to this magic room and they never had to come back into their cage again. They were just gone.

One day a lady came in and asked the people at the pet store if she could see me!!! Me of all puppies, she wanted to see me. I sat up as straight as I could and tried to look as cute as possible. The lady took me into the magic room and watched me walk around and she played with me.

I thought for sure something amazing was about to happen because I had never been in the magic room before. The lady asked one of the people at the pet store how much I cost and they brought in a whole lot of papers. I wasn't sure what was going on but I knew one thing, I was in the magic room. After playing in the room with me for a while the lady picked me up and carried me out the front door of the store. It was working; I was leaving my small cage. I noticed in the lady's hand was a book with a picture on the front that looked like me. I didn't realize I came with an instruction book.

The lady put me in this big thing with wheels. I had ridden in one before when I came to the store. I curled up in the seat and she rubbed my back the whole way home. When we got home she let me out to meet two new dogs. There was a small white fluffy dog that was very grumpy, she called him Mike. There was also a big striped dog that seemed happy to see me, his name was Jack.

The amazing thing was that once I came in the house I found my voice. I could suddenly talk to Mike and Jack.

I could also talk to the lady who brought me there and I call her Mom. Mike introduced himself as the boss of the house. "I can't be bothered with raising a puppy or picking up after one", Mike said. "Give him a break Mike, lighten up, he just walked in the door", Jack entered in my defense. "Well boys lets see, we will need to give your new little brother a name. Hmmm. It needs to be something fitting for a bloodhound and it needs to be short and easy when I call him. Well, any suggestions?' Mike immediately chimed in of course with "big nose, long ears, and drool bucket".

"Okay Mike, that is enough, you need to be nice to your little brother". "How about King Kong" Jack added since that is one of his favorite movies. "No I don't think that will work but thanks for the suggestion Jack. How about Cletus? That's a good country name that is easy to say and it's not very common" "I like it Mom" said Cletus. "Well, that settles it then, from now on you are Cletus. The whole family was happy with the choice, except for Mike, who grumbled to himself and left the room.

- Chapter 2 -
What's a Bloodhound?

That night as I lay in my bed I could not help but think about the puppies at the store and Mike making fun of how I look with the big nose, ears, and feet. I just couldn't get it off of my mind. I decided I would go ask Mom about it, after all she had the instruction book on me. "Mom, I have a question." "Okay Cletus, shoot." "Why do I have such a big nose, ears, and feet? Am I just supposed to be made ugly? The puppies at the store and Mike say that I look weird." "Well, let's look in this book right here and see what the experts say a bloodhound, which is you by the way, is supposed to look like.

It says here you have a long nose because you have an amazing sense of smell, better than other dogs. Bloodhounds have been used for years to find people who are lost, by using their sense of smell. That is something you should be very proud of. As for those long ears of yours they help you smell too." "Mom, that doesn't make any sense". "When bloodhounds are trailing they have their heads down and nose on the ground. Drop your head down Cletus and see what happens. See how your ears drag the ground and flap back and forth? They are bringing the scent from the ground to your nose." "That is cool, boy I'm really built for this finding people thing huh?" "Yes, you are. Your feet are so big because you are going to be big one day. When you grow up into a big dog your feet will be just the right size to hold up your body. God gave you all of your equipment from the beginning, now you just have to grow into it." "Thanks mom, I feel so much better. God really made me special for a special purpose." "Yes he did Cletus, not every dog gets to help people in trouble."

I could hardly sleep that night dreaming about all the wonderful things mom had said bloodhounds could do. I wondered if I would be able to do all of those things. I guess I was off to a good start since I was built for it. Boy, won't Mike be surprised when he sees that I don't just look funny, I have a job. No, Mike probably won't care; he will just make fun of my job. I finally drifted off to sleep dreaming of search dogs, the love for my Mom and brother Jack and yes, the love I felt for my brother Mike.

Several weeks went by and I settled into my new home and family. We had our routines down and everything was going great. I still couldn't help but feel like something was missing. I decided the best thing to do would be to ask my mom what I was forgetting. "Mom, I feel like something is missing in my life. Am I forgetting to do something?" "No, I don't think so Cletus. Maybe now that you have settled in you want to try to do what God made you for, maybe that's why you feel there is an empty hole." "Do you mean being a search dog? Do you really think I could do it? Am I big enough? Am I strong enough? Is my nose big enough? "Okay, one thing at a time. Yes to all of those questions. Now for the hard part, I am going to have to find out what we do to train you to be a search dog. You see Cletus I have never had a search dog, so we will have to learn together. You will have to be patient with me because I might make mistakes, but if you are willing to try your hardest, I will find out what we need to do." "That's a deal!!"

- Chapter 3 -
Search Dog Training Here I Come!

Mom started bringing home books and looking on the computer to try and find out how to make me a search dog. The hard part was there is no one in our area that is doing search dog training. Mom decided our first action would be to go to obedience classes. I was so excited the first day of class I almost had an accident in class but luckily mom recognized the dance I was doing and rushed me outside. I was ready this time when the other puppies in the class made fun of the way I look. A German shepherd said, "Look at your huge nose and ears, how funny looking." I quickly informed him that I needed them for my job. "What job could you possibly do?" "I am going to be a search dog when I grow up!" "Oh, I didn't realize. Sorry." Suddenly I felt so empowered if I had a cape it would have come out like super hound. I really enjoyed obedience class after that was settled and I learned to listen very closely to what my mom said. If I didn't listen I might get hurt or hurt someone by running in the street or playing too rough. Mom was very strict with me but I knew it was because she was making me the best I could be to become a search dog.

After we completed obedience class, with flying colors I might add, Mom decided, that while she looked for a search class to take me to, she could work on my socialization. Boy that is a hard word to say. It just means that I needed to go everywhere in public that I could and be around all kinds of people, so when I started to work none of that would distract me. Socialization training was the best because I got to see people and get lots of love. Mom and I started by going to Lowe's and the playground.

There are a lot of scary noises in Lowe's when you are a puppy. The only thing I really had to work on was the thing with wheels that beeps really loud. Luckily they don't always let it out when I'm there. The playground was great because I got to see kids. I love kids. They are so much fun. Mom also made me climb all over the different things on the playground; she said that works on my coordination. I don't know what that is but I wish it would keep me from falling off the merry-go-round. I got better and better on the playground and my legs grew longer and longer and were getting a little hard to keep under control and under me at times.

My first big adventure happened when it was cool outside. Mom said she was taking me to a new place to practice our socialization. How exciting, I was certainly ready. We drove a long way and got out in a huge parking lot. Well this didn't look very exciting, then a weird looking truck with no windows pulled up and we got on. The truck stopped at this huge entrance crowded with people of all shapes, sizes and ages. This must be a great place; all these people have come to see me today. We walked through the gate and this funny dressed man said, "Welcome to WallyWorld" and he asked me my name.

This place quickly became my favorite place to visit. Mom and I rode the train; we walked all over the park and met people. Most of the people we met thought that we worked for the park. Mom very proudly explained to them that I was a search dog in training and I would stand very tall and stick out my chest every time she said it. Mom and I went to this park several times and every time it was so much fun. We became friends with a lot of the people who work there.

Mom decided we would try some things she had read in one of her books since we couldn't find a search class yet, Mom called it hide and seek. To do this exercise we had to have some help. Mom asked my Aunt Kisy to help us. Aunt Kisy always acts like she doesn't like my drool and dog hair on her but I know she does. Aunt Kisy met mom and me at Grammy's house, because she has a big field behind her house. Aunt Kisy brought one of her socks with her. She would drop the sock and run off and hide. Mom walked me up to the sock and told me to sniff and then find Aunt Kisy. I loved this game. The best part was when I found Aunt Kisy I got to jump on her and she would squeal really loud, like she really liked it, or I think she did.

We played this game a lot. I really felt like I was going to be a search dog one day.

Mom came home from work one day and said that she had a surprise for me. One of the ladies mom works with, Trish, found a camp for us to go to that had a week of search dog classes. I was so excited I didn't know what to do first. Jack was excited for me too, "here's your big break little brother, you can do it." And of course Mike had his opinion, "alright! So drool bucket is going away for a week! That's awesome!" Mom had to explain to Mike that she had to learn too, so she had to go with me. Mike immediately flung himself on the floor and began his fake fit that he throws by pulling on his back leg and growling. Mom reassured him that is wasn't that bad. Mike and Jack would stay in the kennel at the vet's office while we were gone. I couldn't believe it, was I really going to camp to become a search dog. I must have asked mom a million times and every time the answer was yes. My life was now beginning; I was going to be trained for what God made me for.

LaVergne, TN USA
20 January 2011
213266LV00001B